SEALS

(A Fascinating Book Containing Seal Facts, Trivia, Images & Memory Recall Quiz: Suitable for Adults & Children)

By

Matthew Harper

Image Courtesy of mushko

For legal reasons we are obliged to state the following:

Copyright 2013 Matthew Harper

ISBN-13: 978-1497425637

ISBN-10: 1497425638

All rights reserved. No reproduction, copying or transmission of this publication, CD's or DVD included in this system may be made without written permission. No paragraph of this publication may be reproduced, copied or transmitted without written permission, or in accordance with the Copyright Act 1956 (amended).

Hi and a very warm welcome to "Seals".

I'm one of those people who loves to hear about extraordinary facts or trivia about anything. They seem to be one of the few things my memory can actually recall. I'm not sure if it's to do with the shock or the "WoW" factor but for some reason my brain seems to store at least some of it for a later date.

I've always been a great believer in that whatever the subject, if a good teacher can inspire you and hold your attention, then you'll learn! Now I'm not a teacher but the system I've used in previous publications on Amazon seems to work well, particularly with children.

This Seal edition includes a selection of those "WoW" facts combined with some pretty awesome pictures, if I say so myself! At the end there is a short "True or False" quiz to check memory recall and to help cement some of the information included in the book. Don't worry though, it's a bit of fun but at the same time, it helps to check your understanding.

Please note that if you're an expert on seals then you may not find anything new here. If however you enjoy hearing sensational and extraordinary trivia and you like looking at some great pictures then I think you'll love it.

Matt.

I thought that before we get down to some of those amazing seal facts, we might begin with some snapshots of the different types, just to get the juices flowing……….

LEOPARD SEAL

Image Courtesy of kthypryn

HARP SEAL

Image Courtesy of Hugo-photography

NORTHERN FUR SEAL

Image Courtesy of mikebaird

HAWAIIAN MONK SEAL

WEDDELL SEAL

Image Courtesy of Chadica

HARBOR SEAL

NORTHERN ELEPHANT SEAL

Image Courtesy of mikebaird

GRAY SEAL

GALAPAGOS FUR SEAL

Image Courtesy of Crazy Creatures

ANTARCTIC FUR SEAL

Image Courtesy of Liam Quinn

Okay, that's it for the warm up, let's get on with the game......

Image Courtesy of Maw

Did you know that because seals have "winged" or "webbed" fins, they are classified as "Pinniped" animals?

Image Courtesy of jinxmcc

Did you know that the main difference between seals and other marine mammals such as whales and dolphins is that seals give birth on land and not in water?

Image Courtesy of mikebaird

Did you know that seals are believed to have evolved from bear or otter like animals? This might explain why seals cannot breathe under water?

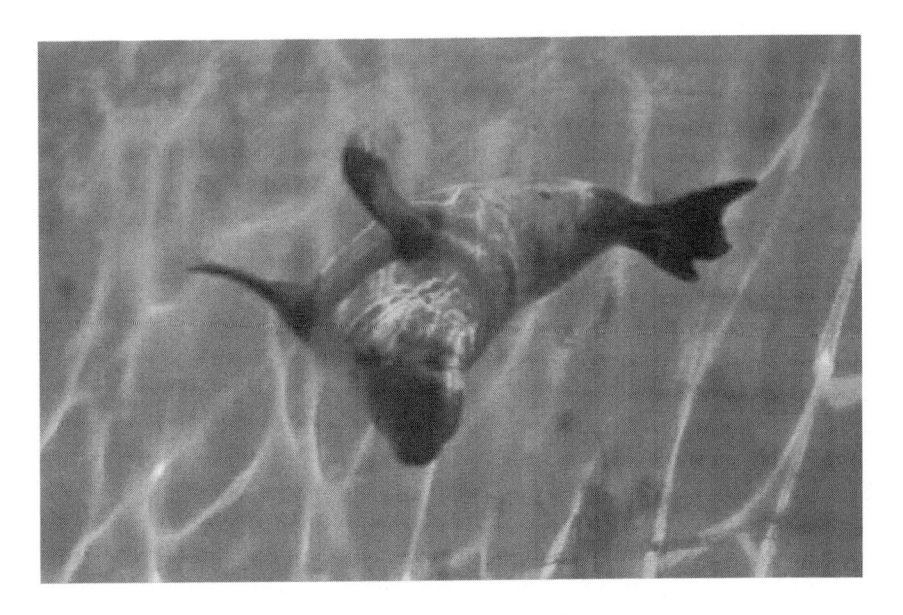

Image Courtesy of City of Albuquerque

Did you know that male seals live around 20 years, while female seals can reach up to 25 years? However, one seal is recorded to have lived 46 years!

Image Courtesy of jomilo75

Did you know that 3 different families exist in the "Pinnipeds" group? These are Phocidae which are true seals; Otaridae which are fur seals and sea lions; and Odobenidae, which are walruses.

Did you know that seals can conserve energy by reducing their heart rate? This is why sleeping seals are often mistaken for being dead.

Image Courtesy of Kiwi Mikex

Did you know that the largest species of seal can weigh up to 2 tons while the smallest species weighs around 65 lbs?

Image Courtesy of docentjoyce

Did you know that a group of seals is collectively known as a herd, pod or strangely, a harem?

Did you know that various species of seals can be found in every ocean of the world and are not only confined to Arctic and Antarctic waters?

Image Courtesy of planetc1

Did you know that there are more than 30 different species of seals?

Image Courtesy of Tambako the Jaguar

Did you know that the largest species of seal is the elephant seal?

Image Courtesy of mikebaird

Did you know that the smallest species of seal is the Galapagos Fur Seal?

Image Courtesy of putneymark

Did you know that Sea Lions and Fur Seals can rotate their hind flippers enabling them to walk on land, which other seals are unable to do?

Image Courtesy of jumpyjodes

Did you know that seals can focus their sight perfectly, both in and out of water?

Image Courtesy of Samuel Mann

Did you know that depending on the species, seals can grow from 1 meter to 5 meters in length?

Image Courtesy of Crazy Creatures

Did you know that seals have the ability to dive to depths of 3000 feet?

Image Courtesy of Genista

Did you know that when seals swim in arctic waters, they restrict blood flow to various body parts to retain body heat?

Image Courtesy of Smudge 9000

Did you know that seals give birth exactly one year apart and generally produce only one pup? This is because the females cannot maintain sufficient blubber supplies to feed more than one pup at a time.

Image Courtesy of Rhys A.

Did you also know that the gestation period of a seal depends on the species but the average is around 9 months?

Image Courtesy of chapmankj75

Did you know that seals are carnivorous? They feed on fish, crustaceans, penguins and other marine life.

Image Courtesy of Callum.H

Did you know that seals generally hold their breath for around 30 minutes when swimming but can last up to 2 hours if necessary when diving for food?

Image Courtesy of Tim Sheerman-Chase

Did you also know that when diving, seals reduce their heart rate to assist with preserving oxygen? At rest, a seal's heart rate is around 112 beats per minute. However, this reduces to an amazing 30/50 beats per minute when diving.

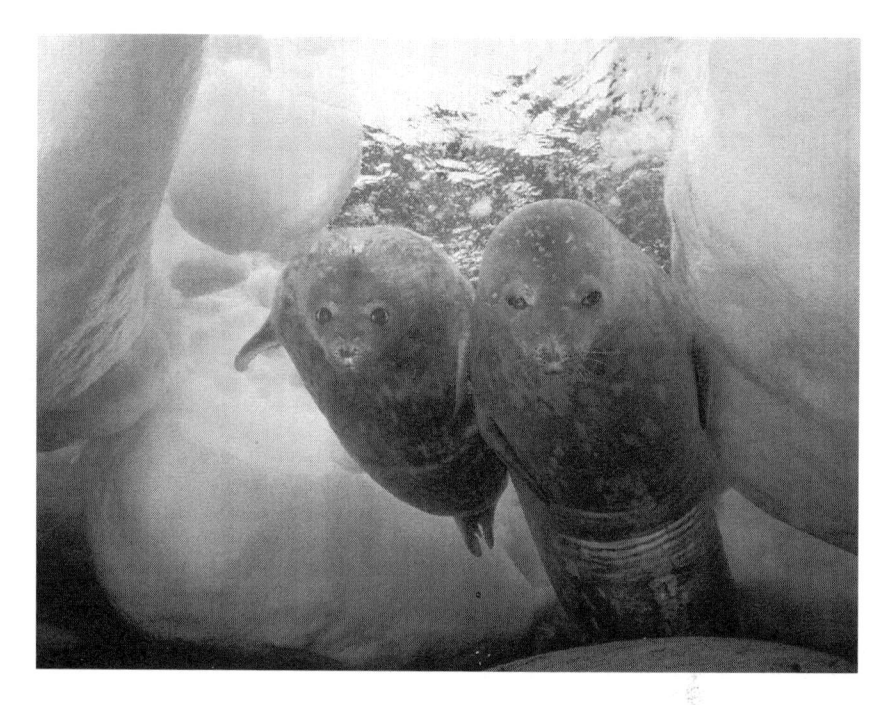

Image Courtesy of changehali

Did you know that female seals do not eat while weaning their pups, which can last for over a month?

Image Courtesy of Blind Grasshopper

Did you know that seals can actually sleep underwater? They can even surface and take breath without awakening from their sleep.

Image Courtesy of Donnaphoto

Did you know that the Leopard Seal actually eats other species of seal?

Image Courtesy of Tambako the Jaguar

Did you know that the milk produced by female seals when feeding their young can contain up to 50% pure fat?

Image Courtesy of mikebaird

Did you know that man hunted the "Caribbean Monk Seal" to extinction? No recorded sighting has occurred since 1952.

Did you know that the Grey Seal population is estimated to be increasing by 7% per annum? However, other seal populations are declining, due to man's intervention including culling in Canada and being hunted for meat and oil.

Image Courtesy of erichhh

Did you know that the virus known as "phocine distemper", killed almost 33% of all common seals in the North Sea in 1988?

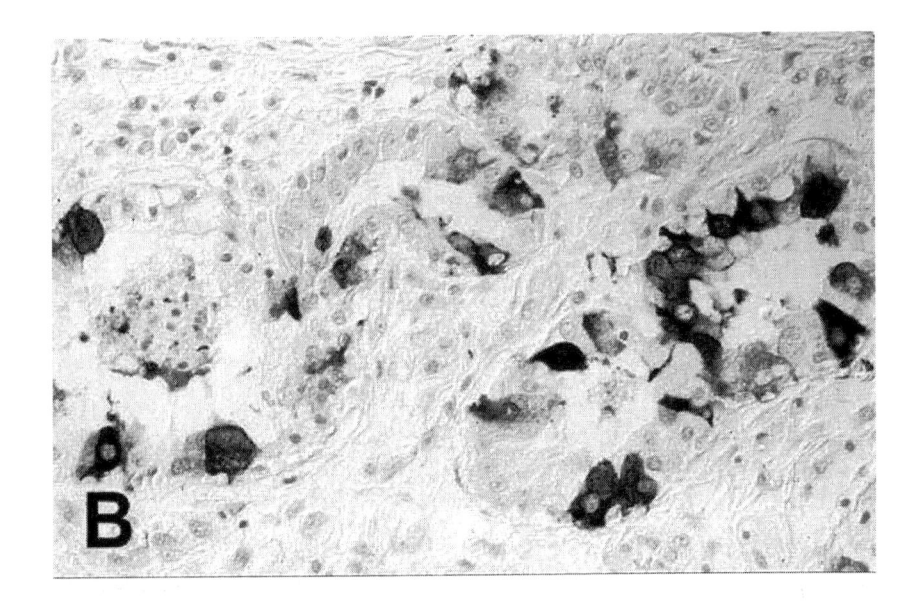

Did you know that seals possess very sensitive whiskers, which help them detect prey in the dark oceans?

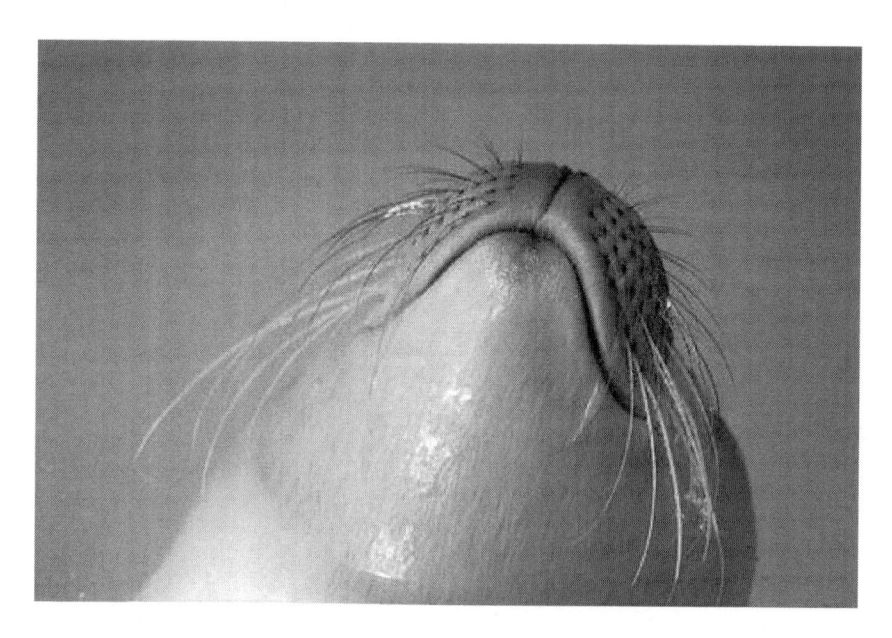

Image Courtesy of zanten.net

Did you know that when seal pups are weaning, they gain around 3/5 lbs per day?

Image Courtesy of SidPix

Did you know that although seals are often mistakenly seen to be crying, they do not have tear ducts?

Image Courtesy of mikebaird

Did you know that the Grey Seal mates on land but the Common Seal mates in water?

Image Courtesy of mikebaird

Did you know that seals often carry parasites which are transferred to fish? One parasite is cod worm which affects the size and quality of cod, so affecting the fishing business.

Did you know that apart from man, the main predators of seals are whales and sharks?

Image Courtesy of hermanusbackpackers

Did you know that seals have little protection from predators so when on land, seals lay very close together for protection? When hunting, seals often hunt in groups.

Image Courtesy of amitp

Did you know that 'Grey Seals' were protected in Britain as early as 1914 and could not be killed between 1 Oct and 15 Dec, (the breeding season)? However, 'Common Seals were not protected until the 1970s.

Image Courtesy of chapmankj75

Did you know that it is estimated, in a colony of birthing seals, almost 15% of pups will die in some way or another?

Image Courtesy of amanderson2

Did you know that when seals are found on land, they are generally breeding or molting? The molting occurs each year and can take up to six weeks to complete.

Image Courtesy of mikebaird

Did you know that the Harbor or Common Seal does not possess external ears? However, the Fur Seal and Sea Lion do possess external ears?.

Image Courtesy of mikebaird

Did you know that the male seal is called a bull, the female a cow and baby seals are called pups?

Image Courtesy of mikebaird

Did you know that seals can hear just as well on land as they can underwater? They are thought to use echolocation, (similar to whales), to navigate.

Image Courtesy of Newtown grafitti

Did you know that the whiskers seals use to detect their prey are called 'vibrissae'?

Image Courtesy of Marcel Burkhard

Did you know that the majority of Grey Seals migrate to Scotland each year to breed?

Image Courtesy of Alexandre Dulaunoy

Did you know that seals have more blood per pound of weight than any other mammal? This allows them to dive to great depths while being protected from the cold.

Image Courtesy of Barbara Walsh Photography

Did you know that before diving, seals form a seal with their nose to prevent seawater entering their bodies, allowing them to navigate underwater for astonishingly long periods?

Image Courtesy of quot;KIUKO&quot

Did you know that a fossil was found in the Canadian Arctic which is thought to have been a walking seal with 4 legs & webbed feet? Experts put the date of the discovery at more than 20 million years ago.

Image Courtesy of Nobu Tamura

Did you know that the "Harp Seal" has a harp-shaped mark in the fur of their flanks & backs, hence the name?

Image Courtesy of Matthieu Godbout

Did you know that seals are not only highly intelligent animals, they are also extremely curious too? They have been known to follow boats for long periods of time just to see what all the fuss is about!

Image Courtesy of john47kent

Did you know that the Leopard Seal is the second largest seal reaching lengths of around 11 feet and weighing up to 1,300 pounds?

Image Courtesy of xeno sapien

That's about it for the seal trivia for now. I'd like to finish this publication with TEN "True or False" questions based on what you've just read. It should help you to really cement the information and to test your memory recall!...
....

DON'T FORGET TO KEEP YOUR SCORE: THERE'S 1 POINT FOR EACH OF THE FIRST 9 QUESTIONS AND 5 POINTS FOR THE BONUS QUESTION GIVING A TOTAL OF 14 POINTS ....

1.

TRUE or FALSE: The main difference between seals and other marine mammals such as whales and dolphins is that seals give birth on land and not in water.

TRUE.

2.

TRUE or FALSE: Seals can conserve energy by reducing their heart rate.

TRUE

3.

TRUE or FALSE: The largest species of seal is the Leopard Seal.

FALSE

The largest species of seal is the ELEPHANT SEAL.

4.

TRUE or FALSE: Seals give birth exactly one year apart and generally produce only one pup.

TRUE

5.

TRUE or FALSE: Female seals do not eat while weaning their pups.

TRUE

6.

TRUE or FALSE: Man hunted the "Hawaiian Monk Seal" to extinction.

FALSE

Man hunted the "CARIBBEAN MONK SEAL" to extinction.

7.

TRUE or FALSE: The Harbor or Common Seal does not possess external whiskers.

FALSE

The Harbor or Common Seal does not possess external EARS.

8.

TRUE or FALSE: Grey Seals migrate to Ireland each year to breed.

FALSE

Grey Seals migrate to SCOTLAND each year to breed.

9.

TRUE or FALSE: Before diving, seals form a seal with their nose to prevent seawater entering their bodies.

TRUE

10.

BONUS ROUND WORTH 5 POINTS

TRUE or FALSE: Grey Seals mate on land but the Common Seal mates in water.

TRUE

Congratulations, you made it to the end!

I sincerely hope you enjoyed my little seal project and that you learnt a thing or two. I certainly did when I was doing the research. Once again, man seems to be the enemy!

ADD UP YOUR SCORE NOW.

1 point for each of the first 9 correct answers plus 5 points for the bonus round giving a grand total of 14 points.

If you genuinely achieved 14 points then you are indeed a

"SEAL MASTER".

8 to 13 points proves you are a "SEAL LEGEND".

4 to 7 points shows you are a "SEAL ENTHUSIAST".

0 to 3 points shows you are a "SEAL ADMIRER".

NICE WORK!

Matt.

Thank you once again for choosing this publication. If you enjoyed it then please let me know using the Customer Review Section through Amazon.

If you would like to read more of my work then simply type in my name using the Amazon Search Box and hopefully you'll find something else that "takes your fancy" or go directly to my website printed below.

Until we meet again,

Matthew Harper

www.matthewharper.info

Image Courtesy of Maw

Printed in Great Britain
by Amazon